Ťhə λNĠƏL ßʌßĬƏS
XVI
Excelsis Deo

Clive Alando Taylor

authorHOUSE

AuthorHouse™ UK
1663 Liberty Drive
Bloomington, IN 47403 USA
www.authorhouse.co.uk
Phone: UK TFN: 0800 0148641 (Toll Free inside the UK)
*   UK Local: (02) 0369 56322 (+44 20 3695 6322 from outside the UK)*

Published by AuthorHouse 08/16/2022

ISBN: 978-1-7283-7483-3 (sc)
ISBN: 978-1-7283-7482-6 (e)

CONTENTS

Angelus Domini

INSPIRIT*ASPIRE*ESPRIT*INSPIRE

Because of the things that have first become proclaimed within the spirit, and then translated in the soul, in order for the body to then become alive and responsive or to aspire, or to be inspired, if only then for the body to become a vessel, or a catalyst, or indeed an instrument of will, with which first the living spirit that gave life to it, along with the merits and the meaning of life, and the instruction and the interpretation of life, is simply to understand that the relationship between the spirit and the soul, are also the one living embodiment with which all things are one, and become connected and interwoven by creating, or causing what we can come to call, or refer to as the essence, or the cradle, or the fabric of life, which is in itself part physical and part spirit.

And so it is, that we are all brought in being, along with this primordial and spiritual birth, and along with this the presence or the origins of the spirit, which is also the fabric and the nurturer of the soul with which the body can be formed, albeit that by human standards, this act of nature however natural, can now take place through the act of procreation or consummation, and so it is with regard to this living spirit that we are also upon our natural and physical birth, given a name and a number, inasmuch that we represent, or become identified by a color, or upon our created formation and distinction of identity, we become recognized by our individuality.

But concerning the Angels, it has always been of an interest to me how their very conception, or existence, or origin from nature and imagination, could have become formed and brought into being, as overtime I have heard several stories of how with the event of the first creation of man, that upon this event, that all the Angels were made to accept and to serve in God's creation of man, and that man was permitted to give command to these Angels in the event of his life, and the trials of his life which were to be mastered, but within this godly decree and narrative, we also see that there was all but one Angel that either disagreed or disapproved with, not only the creation of man, but also with the formation of this covenant between God and man, and that all but one Angel was Satan, who was somewhat displeased with God's creation of man, and in by doing so would not succumb or show respect or demonstrate servility or humility toward man or mankind.

As overtime it was also revealed to me, that with the creation of the Angels, that it was also much to their advantage as it was to ours, for the Angels themselves to adhere to this role and to serve in the best interest of man's endeavors upon the face of the earth, as long as man himself could demonstrate and become of a will and a nature to practice his faith with a spirit, and a soul, and a body that would become attuned to a godly or godlike nature, and in by doing so, and in by believing so, that all of his needs would be met with accordingly.

And so this perspective brings me to question my own faith and ideas about the concept and the ideology of Angels, insomuch so that I needed to address and to explore my own minds revelation, and to investigate that which I was told or at least that which I thought I knew concerning the Angels along with the juxtaposition that if Satan along with those Angels opposed to serving God's creation of man, and of those that did indeed seek to serve and to favor God's creation and to meet with the merits, and the dreams, and the aspirations of man, that could indeed cause us all to be at the mercy and the subjection of an externally influential and internal spiritual struggle or spiritual warfare, not only with ourselves, but also with our primordial and spiritual identity.

And also because of our own conceptual reasoning and comprehension beyond this event, is that we almost find ourselves astonished into believing that this idea of rights over our mortal souls or being, must have begun or started long ago, or at least long before any of us were even souls inhabiting our physical bodies here as a living presence upon the face of the earth, and such is this constructed dilemma behind our beliefs or identities, or the fact that the names, or the numbers that we have all been given, or that have at least become assigned to us, is simply because of the fact that we have all been born into the physical world.

λs even I in my attempts, to try to come to terms with the very idea of how nature and creation could allow so many of us to question this reason of totality, if only for me to present to you the story of the Angel Babies, if only to understand, or to restore if your faith along with mine, back into the realms of mankind and humanity, as I have also come to reflect in my own approach and understanding of this narrative between God and Satan and the Angels, that also in recognizing that they all have the power to influence and to subject us to, as well as to direct mankind and humanity, either to our best or worst possibilities, if only then to challenge our primordial spiritual origin within the confines of our own lifestyles, and practices and beliefs, as if in our own efforts and practices that we are all each and every one of us, in subjection or at least examples and products of both good and bad influences.

Which is also why that in our spiritual nature, that we often call out to these heavenly and external Angelic forces to approach us, and to heal us, and to bless us spiritually, which is, or has to be made to become a necessity, especially when there is a humane need for us to call out for the assistance, and the welfare, and the benefit of our own souls, and our own bodies to be aided or administered too, or indeed for the proper gifts to be bestowed upon us, to empower us in such a way, that we can receive guidance and make affirmations through the proper will and conduct of a satisfactory lesson learnt albeit through this practical application and understanding, if only to attain spiritual and fruitful lives.

As it is simply by recognizing that we are, or at some point or another in our lives, have always somewhat been open, or subject to the interpretations of spiritual warfare by reason of definition, in that Satan's interpretation of creation is something somewhat of contempt, in that God should do away with, or even destroy creation, but as much as Satan can only prove to tempt, or to provoke God into this reckoning, it is only simply by inadvertently influencing the concepts, or the ideologies of man, that of which whom God has also created to be creators, that man through his trials of life could also be deemed to be seen in Satan's view, that somehow God had failed in this act of creation, and that Satan who is also just an Angel, could somehow convince God of ending creation, as Satan himself cannot, nor does not possess the power to stop or to end creation, which of course is only in the hands of the creator.

And so this brings me back to the Angels, and of those that are in favor of either serving, or saving mankind from his own end and destruction, albeit that we are caught up in a primordial spiritual fight, that we are all engaged in, or by reason of definition born into, and so it is only by our choices that we ultimately pay for our sacrifice, or believe in our rights to life, inasmuch that we are all lifted up to our greatest effort or design, if we can learn to demonstrate and to accept our humanity in a way that regards and reflects our greater desire or need, to be something more than what we choose to believe is only in the hands of God the creator or indeed a spirit in the sky.

It was very much my intention not to state the name of any particular place in the script as I thought that the telling of the story of the Angel Babies is in itself about believing in who you are, and also about facing up to your fears. The Angel Babies is also set loosely in accordance with the foretelling of the Bibles Revelations.

I thought it would be best to take this approach, as the writing of the script is also about the Who, What, Where, When, How and Why scenario that we all often deal with in our ongoing existence. It would also not be fair to myself or to anyone else who has read the Angel Babies to not acknowledge this line of questioning, for instance, who are we? What are we doing here? Where did we come from? And when will our true purpose be known? And how do we fulfil our true potential to better ourselves and others, the point of which are the statements that I am also making in the Angel Babies and about Angels in particular,

Is that if we reach far into our minds we still wonder, where did the Angels come from and what is their place in this world. I know sometimes that we all wish and pray for the miracle of life to reveal itself but the answer to this mystery truly lives within us and around us, I only hope that you will find the Angel Babies an interesting narrative and exciting story as I have had in bringing it to life, after all there could be an Angel Baby being born right now.

λfter these things I looked and behold a door standing
open in Heaven and the first voice which I heard was like
a (Trumpet!) speaking with me saying come up here and
I will show you things which must take place after this.

Immediately I was in the spirit and behold a throne set in
Heaven and one sat on the throne and he who sat there was
like a Jasper and a Sardius Stone in appearance, And there
was a Rainbow around, In appearance like an Emerald.

Time is neither here or there, it is a time in between time as it is the beginning and yet the end of time. This is a story of the Alpha and the Omega, the first and the last and yet as we enter into this revelation, we begin to witness the birth of the Angel Babies a time of heavenly conception when dying Angels gave birth to Angelic children who were born to represent the order of the new world. The names of these Angel Babies remained unknown but they carried the Seal of their fathers written on their foreheads, and in all it totalled one hundred and forty four thousand Angels and this is the story of one of them.

Excelsis Deo

Inspirit * Aspiré * Esprit * Inspiré

Sánctus *Hosánna * Glória * In Excélsis Deo

ΩΜƎGΛ.XVI

THE BEGINNING OF OMEGA: TIME
λ.Ω PROΛRKHÉ THE ΛRKHÉ 1.É.Ð

λs such are the perpetuities unending, an enduring abundance, arising out of the kinship of an unbridled love, forces of nature, upon unlimited horizons, endless resources, for what we reap is what we sow, and yet time lays silently sleeping, as the sowing and reaping seems to carry on, but time can be so deceiving, by playing possum all along, for the reaping is the harvest of heaven, now sown upon the earth below, and yet who could dream of such a time, when time is all but invisible.

λs old as time itself may be, formed from the beyond, issuing forth, until all things new are begotten and yielded unto themselves, as much as time is a timeless anomaly, giving chase to hasten the winds, and yet no one knows how time began and yet no one knows if time will ever end, just like the never ending rearranging of time, and yet without such signs, how could we know, or even discern ourselves from it, and yet throughout the changing of time, nothing seems to change at all.

λnd yet from where do all things come, if not from the genesis of creation, and yet still, all things have not become fashioned or formed, and yet because of time I am born and called into existence, and yet what if I told you, that you are born of the place that you are going too, and what if I told you, that you are born of the place from which ye' have departed, and what if I told you, that not only are you born of the roots within this land, but ye' are also born upon the ground, upon which ye' now stand.

λuthor
T.I.M.E – Thoughts Inside My Existence

THE VISION OF: HEAVEN AND EARTH
λ.Ω CΛLÉNDΛR YÉΛR 1.É.Đ

λs much as the latter part of the previous age had eventfully come to pass, still it remained that humankind would have to live within the aftermath, of a nocturnal and desolate separation, from the Heavens above the Earth, as there was a time of Angelus E' Nocturnālis whereupon the age of this separation had signified the end of a spiritual life.

λs it was throughout this period, and without God's presence to guide us, that what was inevitably to come, to take its' place, was the beginning of the age of the iconoclastic beasts, that had readily come prepared to inflict their judgments of war upon the Earth, as it was during this period of darkness, that would eventually come to fulfil a nocturnal and prophetic separation between humankind and God.

λnd yet for those of us who had come to survive these events, would also have to come to endure, and to somehow persevere through the remnants of a desolate and barren land, that was by now only partially inhabitable, as unbeknown to us at the time, we would later come to realize that within the aftermath of this war of separation, that the protective layer of our atmosphere that had shielded us from the effects of radiation, had by now become irreparably damaged and affected by the protractions of this iconoclastic war.

For even unto the celestial heavens along the celestial equator, did they cover the whole of the entire earth, like a blanket of infinite light casting its' purest glow, that it shone its' illuminations across the breadth, of what was once such a natural and organic ecosystem, of a living and breathing and yet fruitful planet, which was by now being made readily prepared for its' divine transformation.

λnd so it was that Angels of the celestial abode, and now also those of Empyreans, had descended upon the earth in their many forms, and gathered up all of that which was the natural substance formed within the spirit of Humankind, and of that with which was therein to be saved from the decays of this plagued and dying world, as the world was not sought out to be destroyed, but instead to be renewed in all of its glory and splendour, but as it stood that there was to be no living soul left upon its inhabitancy to witness the renewal of creation.

For no one should be able to speak of it, nor offer up any account of it, or for any other such reason, be able to speak of it, or for any such act of influence, cause God, who in having no allies or partners, would give be aligned to any such reasons of definition of explanation, in being the omnipotent force, that upon this one divine cause, would influence his elect to carry out this one singular motion of divinity.

λlbeit that that this eternal living spirit, would be caused to move once more over the darkness of the earth, if only to reshape and to reform its' destiny, and to make it become ever more abundantly filled with the simplest of precious life, which would be done, and only in accordance, with the divine the presences of none else, except and other than, that of the Archangels, that is Gabriel and Michael and Raguel and Raphael and Remiel and Uriel and Zerachiel.

A B C D E F G H I J K L M
Z Y X W V U T S R Q P O N
λ.Ω CALÉNDAR YÉAR 1.É.Đ

λccording to the lost records of the Gregorian calendar, the year was approximately 3240 A.D, and all that which has been prophesied, had already come to pass, as Humankind itself had by now become dispersed amongst the planets and the stars, seeking out new planets to inhabit. As it was now the age of the Omega, and all that could be gathered and recorded, before such an age had fully come into being, was also limited, as there was very little known about the digitally recorded and invaluable information, that could be researched, reviewed and relied upon so as to inform us of any immediate progress.

λs the last known updates regarding the Dome in the history of the Earth were kept and recorded by the one and only known Elder, as being registered as none other than Obadiah 144, during the period of this age. Although it was through these newly implemented belief systems, that were by now of a diminished nature, due to the reality, and the fact that life had by now become expired, or was almost at the point of extinction, and so within this new automated and technological world, whereupon humankind were all but being wiped out, that there was no real way of knowing how Humanity could or would one day return to repopulate the Earth once again.

From out of the dark matter of the thermosphere, did an infant seemingly appear from out of the nothingness, surrounded by the luminous glow of a halo, now descending down towards us, in becoming more apparent whilst materializing forth from above the Kármán line, as we also looked into the vast distance, towards a procession of Angels, who were by now ascending higher and higher away from the earthly realm of the Dome, albeit with the exception of one Angel that had broken ranks and departed away from the flock, and began heading in our direction, as we were yet to comprehend, what it was that we were witnessing here, except that the glow that once surrounded and dominated the Dome was no longer to be seen, and so we could only conclude that the Earth as we knew it was no more.

As much as the stark choice was clear, that either we were to follow a path into the void of the unknown, or otherwise, we were to prepare towards fulfilling our own prophetic destiny, which would, or could be proven to be a legacy as foretold by the greatest of all Humankind, or we could, within our own free will, maintain a level of unsurrendered control over our own indeterminate future, albeit with the momentum and the uncertainty towards an unpredictable and yet unforeseeable outcome, if only our knowledge beyond all definition of comprehension, would permit it to be so.

As it was either this or that, whereby we could otherwise follow a path of the forever faithful, whereby many are called and yet few are chosen to face the greatest challenges of our lives, set against the backdrop of such a vast revelation, despite the inevitability of what this path, of the chosen had already predicted itself to be, and yet by definition, why would we choose to otherwise deviate from such a path, that would forever be coming into its' own, and yet why should we not try to rely upon our own emboldened hopes and interpretations of Humankind along with the aspirations of a world that is yet to be born, as such are the feet made of sand and clay, from which all living things are made to take on their shape and form within the creation.

THE WAY OF THE WORLD: TO COME
λ.Ω HΛLΛHKHΛ ΘLΛM HΛ-BΛ 1.É.Đ

λs a fleet of w.o.r.ships set sail across the vast expanse, of an unbounded and uninterrupted void of dark matter, watching and waiting in anticipation, for any unusual and abstract objects of activity, moving across the surface of a once long ago inhabited and now desolate and abandoned planet.

Ferrying passengers and cargo high above the Earths exosphere, voyaging through the invisible boundary line, upon the edge of space, whereupon a capable and ample number of un-quantified spacecrafts, are scattered like flashing stars in atmospheric spaceflight.

Floating upon an immense, and yet boundless and seamless empty void, like artificial satellites stationed around the planet, whilst encircling the globe and observing the infinite space for any arising anomalies, whilst regularly transmitting and receiving updated intervals of audio signals of relative and translative records of information.

Updating and determining, the present coordinates and the positions, from a uniquely relayed computational data system of multiple and varied languages, from one vessel to another, whilst identifying and charting the journeying of other spacecrafts and vessels around the Earth.

λuthor
L.I.G.H.T – Life Is Giving Hope Today

UNITED ORBITAL SPACE STATION
ALTITUDE: 400 KM - ORBIT SPEED: 17500-MPH

MOON OUTPOST: Computer Systems Scroll Down And Select From Database, Past And Current Ship Positions For Almost Every Vessel In The World, **Data Logger:** Monitoring Current Terrestrial Ship Positions Tracking From Mothership, **OMEGA: W.O.R.SHIP – VESSEL 3240**

Data Logger: Receiving Cargo, Reported, Docking At United Orbital Space Station, Carrying Vital Supplies, **PROVIDENCE: W.O.R.SHIP– VESSEL 3410**

λs I do not say these things lightly, nor do I say these things to trivialize such matters of great importance, and yet with a fair and just attitude please do not take it upon yourself, to forsake all others, or to be the sake of any cause, that may be of a detrimental hindrance even unto yourselves.

For as much as we learn to consider, and to take account of all of the external influences and elements, that are often found to be influencing our aspectual awareness, and also in knowing that these energies are constantly ebbing and flowing and pressing upon the psyche, whilst also making an impression and impact, upon the susceptibility of our very own human nature.

For as much as we may be under the influence of the stars in heaven and as much as we may wonder in awesome glory as we gaze upon them from afar, with such amazement, and yet even we within the inquisitive nature of our own curiosity, are left to speculate and to question, and to marvel at the simplest and yet the most majestic of all miracles within this creation, which is a resurrected world created for all sentient beings.

THE SKY WORLD: HEAVEN
λ.Ω ÉΛRŤH 1.É.Đ

λlthough there are worlds
within this world
still the Earth remains the same

λlthough there is an underworld
within this world
still the Earth remains the same

λlthough there are principalities
and powers to rule this world
still the Earth remains the same

λlthough there are dreams
within the dream world
still the Earth remains the same

λlthough there are spirits
within the spirit world
still the Earth remains the same

λlthough the world has a past
a present and a future
still the Earth remains the same

λuthor
E.A.R.T.H – Every Angel Returns To Heaven

λs the Earth upon reflection, from the various occupied outposts, albeit from a united orbital space station, and also that of an allied collective colonial homestead structures, of habitable bases constructed upon the Moon, appeared to glow, albeit for a moment in time, like a shining blazing star, although it was unclear of what was taking place upon its' surface, due to the intensity of this luminous and yet strangely brilliance of a glow, as even the atmosphere itself, seem to take on another odd and yet surprisingly infectious and overwhelming feeling or force of purity, as if to transform metabolically deep beneath the metaphysical state that we found ourselves in, albeit that it remained indifferent to our own consciousness, and yet was somewhat unexplainable and yet effortlessly enhancing our innate and natural abilities.

λs the Dome had remained in this state for approximately two hundred and forty-one aeons, although none would have thought, or even understood that what had come to pass was perhaps the inevitable end of creation itself, or that perhaps what we were seemingly experiencing, was the last few remaining moments of our very own mortality and re-birth simultaneously, even inasmuch, that we could not truly account for, nor did we realize how we had become changed by this phenomena, except that in realizing seamlessly, that a child does not witness its' own birth, and yet it is born.

λs so it was also that our very own transformation did similarly take place, that upon in such a way, and notably so, that we did also begin to comprehend this, by the responses of our cries, as if we had leapt out of our decaying bodies and yet instantly inherited new ones, fashioned and renewed out of our very own begotten forms, and yet the glowing light that had engulfed and surrounded the Dome, was becoming more and more apparent, in that now it appeared to be emanating from an infinite number of Angels, that had circled and descended upon the Earth, and yet the World and the Earth were not of the same thing.

MOON-OUTPOST HOMESTEAD INTEL-CIRCULAR: RESPONSE TO UNITED ORBITAL SPACE STATION
λ.Ω ÉPIQUE REQUIÉM 1.É.Đ

Who doth but take delight in the accusations of the accursed, reveling in the pitiful deprivations of the suffering, dancing in the debauchery of such human decline, indulging in the pleasures of such vile and vitriolic charm, Feeding upon the weaknesses of the afflicted, making a mockery in the face of truth, sustained by the gratifications of violence and temper, bolstered by the acts of innate evils.

Relishing in the blame of ruinous conflict as an advocate for destruction and desolation, acting as a trickster and deceiver of the hearts and minds of humankind, a partaker in planting the seeds of destruction, acting as a conjurer and a menace, equally in knowing, that upon this reckoning, how the beloved doth knoweth thee.

λnd yet because of such things, we are disconnected, and because of such objects, we are systematically affected, and because of such materialism, we are disaffected, and because of such abstractions, we are obstructed, and because of such boredoms, we are wanting.

λnd because of such lies, we are loathing, and because of such inertia, we are corrupted, and because of such structures, we are breaking, And because of the mechanical, we have lost our nature, and because of such technological advances, the question pertains to ask, are we in need of savior, for love hath not only conquered religion, but has also overcome the pillars that have kept us apart.

λuthor
H.O.M.E – Heaven Offers Many Examples

Data Logger: Vessels Of Unknown Types, Passenger Capabilities 115,200,000+, Are As Unspecified, Coordinates from Transponder Is Not Setup With Correct Information, Enabling Transponder – First Maiden Voyage Vessel To Embark Recorded As **ARC SURVIVAL: W.O.R.SHIP – VESSEL 2999**

Data Logger: Ship Is Not Complying With Any Provisionary Particulars,

Vessel Appears To Be Adrift With Many Years Of Fuel Usage, Machinery Problems, Capacity Including Latest Intel, **Crew** Of Over **800+**

As in the absence of any universal peace, and yet in the times of such great wars, and in such an era of worldly troubles, then who amongst us would act to intercede upon our behalf, and who would come forth to instruct us in our many ways, if only to protect the young and the old and the meek and the feeble, and who would come forth, to act as an advocate upon our behalf, for those of us who are opposed to such acts of confrontation.

And yet for those of us, who are not prepared for the perils of this journey ahead, then who would best be suited to act as our guide, to lead us from out of our tribulations, as surely we should seek to fill this void with praise and worship, and surely we should fill this void with prayers of reverence in asking for mercy, instead of waiting for it to become a desolate place full of nothingness.

And yet as it may stand, then who would be concerned, if not the strong and the mighty, or the rich and the wealthy, or of those of us who could afford to flee from such an apocalyptic judgment of finality, then who would come forth to help the weak and the poor, and those of us who are left to suffer and to endure the end of all ages, and yet was it not the faithful amongst the faithless, who would first be called up to the heavens, surely in knowing that upon this divine account, could only serve to open up the eyes and the hearts and the minds of all humankind.

OBADIAH 144 - LAST DIGITAL ANGEL DOME MESSAGE: RECORDED APPROXIMATELY 2999 A.D
λ.Ω ŤHE ŤEMPLÉ 1.É.Ð

I am close to the temple

λs I present myself to the temple

I am besides the temple

λs I reside in the temple

λs I kneel an' pray inside the temple

As the temple houses me

λs I make my offering inside of the temple

λs I come before the altar of the temple

λs I am altered inside of the temple

λs I am changed inside of the temple

λs I am renewed inside of the temple

λs I take refuge inside of the temple

λs I give praise an' worship inside of the temple

λs I make the temple my sanctuary

Until I am delivered

For the sanctity of the temple.

Is there some way of knowing, or accepting such a thing, as inescapable truth, and yet even if we are somewhat uniformed, or unaware of such profound and yet relative information, albeit that it may be beneficial to one's own reasoning, and even if we did not know, then how could it possibly affect us, or is this just a myth, that ignorance is bliss, and so therefore can only naively serve to protect us from such a looming fate, simply because we were to admit in saying, that we did not know.

Or is it that we are only seemingly unprepared for what was, or what is about to happen, and even if we did have some minor understanding, or inkling about it, albeit with an added element of skepticism, but even then how could we prepare and defend ourselves against it, if something that is said to be so finite, within its' fullest measure, that even in our own estimates and doubts, how could we even know to accept, or even reject it.

λs we all eventually have to come face to face within our own limited capacity, along with the entities born out of our own insecurities, even when our own vulnerabilities are exposed, now leaving us bare, with nothing, and nowhere to turn too, other than that which may turn out to be born out of our own delusions, as such is the measure of the bravest and yet the faintest of hearts, that even faith and love and compassion, would either flee, or find us in such a state of grace, if not upon the recognition of our own acceptance, and yet upon its' appearance, is not the end the only true and sincere finality of completeness, as such as we may find within the Earths story, are only the causes that separate fact from fiction.

Surely it has been presented to one and all, that we, and upon its' delivery, expected to receive a message of wonderment, and a message of betterment, and a message of enlightenment, and yet unexpectedly we are fearfully reminded of why all these things pertaining to this world are impermanent and temporary, and imminent, and yet all that we could have imagined, has not yet managed to move us away from our stubborn and dogged and obstinate ways.

And yet further still, even with this idle and indolent and trifling behavior, which has disconnected and obscured our sights, and cut us off from one another, and blinded us away from witnessing all that could be regarded as being both just and fair and poured out upon a wholly conscientious mind, that is born from the nature of the Holy Spirit. Even if such ideas are proven to be of no use, to those of whom are self seeking, through their own conceited arrogance and ambitions, to challenge the very essence of life itself, then please bare with me for one precious moment within this infinite circle of time, in acknowledging and in understanding, and in accepting, that all these things, that have already come to pass are by no means immaterial, or accidental, or inconsequential.

For as much as it may be inconvenient, or uncomfortable, or even unacceptable to those of whom do not take delight within this truth nor do they share in the joy of this faith, nor do they take any pleasure in this wise counsel, nor do they seek such desires of aspirations. And yet for all the things that have been fought for and brought forth into this world was always but a sign of the times, if only to remind us, that for all things to become fulfilled, then all things however remote, and all things however unfathomable, and all things however unexpectedly, shall reign down upon us all, even as we are encouraged to keep watch and to be vigilant, and even as we are urged to meditate and to pray with an unwavering and steadfast and immovable mind, as much we are inspired to fix our gaze upon the heavens above.

UNITED ORBITAL SPACE STATION CIRCULAR: TO MOON-OUTPOST INTEL-OBSERVATION OMEGA λ.Ω THE PÉNIŤENT MΛN 1.É.Đ

λs to the reverence of whom I owe an unending apology, for thinking that I could be attributed, if only to be made so perfect in the fullness of time, and yet instead, only to realize that I would be made to feel so deeply sorry, in knowing that I would not, nor could not afford to fulfill such an endeavor of hope, within these endless pursuits of a relationship with love, and yet as I understand that to be made whole, requires a contrite heart that can only then, be made ready and prepared to receive such compassion and forgiveness.

If only wanting for the future to be made present, and for the present to become fulfilled, and for the fulfillment to be made perfect and true, and yet because I truly know that in all else, that even if I had failed at the very beginning of this journey, even before I had truly started out upon seeking such a divine acceptance, if only to encompass, and to challenge all the things that were set before me, and yet as much as I may owe you, still I know that this much, is much more than my heart can muster, and yet further still I know, that it is not yet enough to fully recompense and repay all that I owe, upon the solemn gravity and weight of this simple life.

λnd yet however unintentional, whenever you hurt someone, you also hurt yourself, as surely when someone hurts you, then they too, are also affected by the nature of their actions, as such is the human connection that ties us all together, as it is also in situations of confrontation, whereby we are physically, or mentally challenged, that naturally we may feel remorse, or become upset, or aggrieved, or emotionally disturbed, or disempowered, simply because of the energy or the spiritual exchange that takes effect from the exchange of any altercation, which also impacts, and results upon us in a negative way.

As it is also this same feeling that stems from being tricked or deceived, which also affects us in a similar way, except that it only serves to diminish the very nature of our human spirit, as such are the processes of dealing with, or learning to heal our inner souls, from such a feeling of wrongdoing against a fellow human being, as it is also this emotion that has caused us to feel, as if we had fallen from grace and into sin, for as much as it may be right versus wrong, which is also at the very core of human nature, then so too must it also be a fundamental building block of truth, that is at the very heart of our personal and spiritual growth.

For as much as sorrow begets a debt of regret, which is the human cost of hurting those of whom we should truly love, and yet fail too, as such as it is duly noted, that upon our flaws and defects, that such is the depth and depravity, of torment and misery, that in such a vain hope, we would hope that we could be forgiven, and yet would forgiveness be enough, to cover or to conceal this human feeling of guilt, even if the pain caused, was unintended, but nevertheless, the sin was already committed, and so the repentance must begin, as so too must the inward journeying of accepting one's own shortcomings, if only in the sincere desire to break free from the shame and the pain unduly caused out of error.

As within the measures of time, I can only but learn to surrender such attitudes as adopted by the nature of my character, even when such impressions would suggest, that even if I was to portray the gravest of such defective errors, that in time, I hoped could be addressed by such a modest and yet divine spirit, and yet in entertaining such ideas, and in thinking that I could become much more, other than what I am, if only to be made readily acceptable within thy sight, a dimly lit shining light, dying to love and to cherish, and yet in pleading to think, that I should not stop believing, in such a perfect and true love, through the outpouring of his wisdom and the beloved compassion of that which is Jesus Christ.

Author
H.E.L.P – Help Every Living Person

As it was revealed to me, so then shall I reveal it to you, that upon your birth into this world, that God would send an Angel to watch over you and to see, that you would come to no harm, an Angel, that would guide you, and protect you, as you slept, as you arose, and yet as you were unknowingly surrendered into its' care and keeping, up until the last day of your life, in that this abiding Angel, was instructed to give a full account of your life, as you stood in the presence of the Almighty.

So it would seemingly reveal, that this spirit, which had once ignited and sparked the soul, upon a body cloaked and laden with flesh and blood has now found the desire to set itself free, from the restrictive confinements of such a mortal and yet decaying and temporary form and yet not without an endless struggle, and not without such a violent resistance to keep all else at bay, whilst being tied to its fleshy embodiment, if only in seeking to keep itself from the release and the liberation of its' truest form upon its' own emancipation.

Even inasmuch, that such was the sin, that did seep deep within, in seeking to corrupt all that was once made to be wholly innocent, and wholly pure, was now spreading like a cancer, consuming the very nature of the mind, and the body, and the soul, if only to infectiously take root in cutting off all the channels that make up the arteries, whereupon the life-force of such energies would naturally ebb and flow, much like the streams flowing into the rivers, and much like rivers finding their way to the sea, until all that is divided, becomes divinely united with one and all.

And yet the streams, and the rivers, and the seas are no more, inasmuch, that we have substituted something real, for something synthetic, as we have also traded in something natural for something artificial, even as the earth had once began to rage with the echoes and screams of such injustices, but little did we do to listen to its' predictions and warnings for the promises that were once made.

And yet were by now all completely broken, and yet unwillingly, she did not give up, but had to be aided, albeit somewhat reluctantly if only destined to accept, and to resign herself to the prophetic realities of her own climatic fate.

However we imagine it, still it cannot be imagined, and however we predict it, still it remains unpredictable, and however we describe it, still it remains indescribable, and whatever we thought we knew about it, still we know nothing at all, and yet still we see how heaven has reigned down upon from such a high place.

And yet still we do not know from which place it reigns down, and as much as every soul is stirred by it, and as much as every spirit is ignited by it, still we cannot begin to explain the whys and the wherefores, as quite simply it is put, that it is not of this world, but of another, and it is not of this life, but of the next.

Once we begin to imagine things, should we imagine them as they are, or as they were, or how they could be, and once we begin to dream of such things, do we dream of them as they are, or as we recollect them, or do we dream of them as in ways unexplained, and yet, once we begin to imagine and dream of other worlds, such as Heaven upon the Earth, how can we truly know if such unimaginable dreams ever come true.

AN ACT OF: GOD
λ.Ω ΘΜΝΙΤ̆ΈΜΡΘΡΛΛ 1.É.Đ

What if you could save the world, and yet in spite of that you couldn't save yourself, as much as history is full of such stories of heroics that speak of the ultimate self-sacrifice, even as much to say that no man hath than this, that a man lay down his life for his friends, or even that a parent in the act of unconditional love would sacrifice everything so that their children may continue to live on. As such is the transferring of one's souls energies into the next, inasmuch that even as your parents had also channeled their energies into you, and so on and so forth from one generation unto another.

λs it is through this medium of such a natural process, whereupon we begin to understand, why one would refrain, and yet the other hastens, albeit from a viewpoint of being self-centered, towards becoming selfless, and yet also from a perspective of being inwardly, towards reaching for a more reciprocal attitude of openness, and yet further still, to shift ones dogmatic opinions towards a more noble sense of godliness, and yet to forsake the world is to embrace the Father, and yet to save the world, is to sacrifice yourself, and yet within such a selfless act, could you, or would you beget heaven itself.

λuthor
S.O.S – Save Our Souls

Data Logger: Evaluating The Mechanical Integrity Core Of The Maiden Voyage Ship **ARC SURVIVAL: W.O.R.SHIP – VESSEL 2999**, Sweeping Analysis, Its' Purpose, To Help Ensure Continuation Of Species, Automative Controls On All Vessels Fully Active, And All Life Support Systems Fully Functional.

Data Logger: Observing Geo-location **YIN YANG: W.O.R.SHIP – VESSEL 3829**, Current Position N.S 43 Degrees, Providing Logistical Support, And Enabling Critical Resources To All Ship Systems.

Data Logger: Further Monitoring Scanner Analysis Detects Over **6,239,000+** Other Unknown Terrestrial Positions Of Ships Of Various Types, Also Showing Those Of Other **W.O.R.SHIPS**, Including Passengers That Departed And Arrived At Various **HOMESTEAD OUTPOSTS**, Upon The Imminent Brink Of Mass Extinction.

MOTHERSHIP CIRCULAR: RE-ENTRY TO PLANET EARTH: MOTHERSHIP OMEGA: W.O.R.SHIP – VESSEL 3240
λ.Ω HUMΛNIŤIÉS 1.É.Đ

The Earth is a living organism, so please remember that before you to start to plunder its' resources, as we're only acting like parasites, feeding off the back of creation, as you're only keeping pace with the whole of the human race before you've even started to run your marathon race, but remember its' only a walk in the park if you want to see the whole of the excursion.

λs in the days of the Empire, it was empirical, as the facts coincide in line with the truth, as we emancipate beneath the weight of the imperial state, but tell me what would you do, before you're born again, to make amends, standing in front of the Emperor and Empress.

The extraterrestrial inquisitive ancestor, the revelation of secrets from another Dome, as the diamonds and pearls in a post-modern world, are the resources of an ancient civilization, but now the end is nigh, as we complete the story, as the estimated clock out time is predicted to be, three thousand and two hundred and forty.

λuthor
H.O.P.E – Heaven Offers People Eternity

λs what was to follow moments later from out of the dark denseness of this now dying and deceased planet, was that a sentient angelic like Being, that had broken away from the flock, had appeared to us, and was by now travelling at speed towards our direction, and yet the closer it came, the more brilliantly and brightly it shone, upon bearing a Celestial Angelic dazzling Aura, although by now it was ascending directly and upwardly upon its' approach, towards engaging with the glowing Halo of what appeared to be the embodiment of a sentient infant Child, as it was upon their engagement with one another, that they did begin to make their way towards the exosphere, which was far beyond the geocorona and the orbit of the Moon.

λs within our immediate observations, we simply watched in suspense as they flew by, until the occurrence of some other strange phenomenon began to take effect, as it was through the interactions of their respective Halo and Celestial Aura, which begin to merge as one, as if somehow they had connectedly combined together in producing a mass surge of fusion and energy.

λs also within their acknowledgement, did they appear to beckon towards us from afar, as we watched on in amazement, at how their interactions had caused, or prompted the edges of the geocorona to recede back, layer by layer, like a rolled up scroll, as the Planets, and the Heavens, and the Earth were removed from our sights, until all had become vanquished,

And yet in its' place did a new Earth seemingly begin to form and appear, as it was also that this newly created Earth, was called and brought forth, so as to be fashioned from out of the Dome of its' former creation, as it was this mystery of creation itself that had begun, by the unraveling threads of time, whereupon the angelic infant child and the celestial Angel, had by now, indicated and directed for us to enter therein.

And so we made our way, by the means through a portal that had now opened up, in presenting us with the opportunity to venture therein, if only to be presented thereupon with the dimensions of a whole new Earthly domain, and yet, if this is where it was all to begin, then why did it all have to end so profoundly, and yet even by that estimate, still everything around us had already begun to fall into complete alignment with itself.

□ ▽ MΛN-WΘ-MΛN ▽ ○
♂ MALE-FE-MALE ♀ HERMAPHRODITE ☿

Λs the nearest star was much too far for us to settle down upon its' surface, and the satellite was much too bright for us to see our own lives in reflection, as we travelled beyond the sea of tranquility, loving every emotion, harvesting the pearls of a derelict world, the visionary and the Captain.

Λfter the Moon way beyond the Dunes, it always seemed that we kept on searching, for a distant place for the human race, now that the Earth was abandoned and deserted, so we sent a probe to find a new hope, another life-form to feed the hungry.

Into that void, was another Sky world, and all of those who went before us, and yet beyond the hype we set our sights upon the journey of a true discovery, to take our place into outer space, it was the Genesis of another story.

Λuthor
L.I.F.E – Liberty Is For Everyone

OMEGA EARTH RECORDS: 3240 THE MACHINE SINNED
λ.Ω CΛLENDΛR YEΛR 1.É.D

In the beginning was the machine, the man made machine, and the machine had complete control over man and his dominion, and man's dependency upon the machine was one of absolute submission, as man had thought not to question the machines influence, or control over his life. As man's autonomy was one of complete reliance upon the machine, as man could not function without first consulting and engaging with the machine first, although during this period in the advances of the machines that man himself had invented, as there was a disconnect from mans eventful past, that man could not account for, and because of the machines domination, man just accepted that this was the way of all things.

λlthough there was a time long, long, ago before the machines, that man was once visited by a group of Sky Beings, that lived and resided with man, in order for man to develop and to grow and to learn more about himself and his environment, as this was a time before the machines had become dominant, and the land was plentiful and fruitful, and man and his wo-man lived in complete harmony with himself, and also with these Beings of the Sky world, which nurtured and helped him to thrive and to develop his natural talents and abilities.

λs it was after a thousand years, that these Beings from the Sky world had helped man to reach his full conscious and spiritual maturity, so as to understand his relationship with all things, and to comprehend himself and the environment within which he had inhabited, as the Beings from the Sky world were quite simply of an extraordinary and different nature to man, and did not wish, or desire to overly exert their will or their influences over the desired freedoms of man.

And so it was that once the thousand years had expired, so it was that these enlightened Sky Beings had to return to their home-world amongst the stars and the heavens, high above mans dominion, which even man himself recognized as the Sky world, as man and his wo-man also knew and understood that these Sky Beings were also an extension of themselves, and for a period of time, man did not think to question his relationship with the Beings of the Sky world.

As it was during the absence of the Sky world Beings, that man was quite content with himself and his wo-man, and they and their children and their grand-children, also had good and fulfilling lives, until there came a time, when the man and the wo-man had grown apart from the Beings of the Sky world, and had forgotten about their fundamental teachings that had once served to keep man and his wo- man happy and contented and fulfilled, and yet as the generations came to pass, man became curious about the stories and the mysteries surrounding the Sky world Beings, and how they might one day reach it.

And so there came a time when man set about building machines that would one day help him to accomplish such a task, except that it would take man an even longer period of time to complete such a task, due to the lack of his own knowledge, which was limited in line with the generations that had followed, as man had only a thinly veiled and slimly limited understanding of what the Sky world Beings had previously shared and taught to man during their thousand year reign, and so with such limited ability, he began to build his machines, based upon his only ambition of once again reaching the Sky world.

λs mans technological advance was slow but steady, and so overtime man had accomplished his task of building such a machine that could effectively assist him in applying his strategies to any and everything, except that the machines would need to be updated and improved upon regularly, so much so, that in its' design and advancement, man had now come to rely upon the machine in place of his own independent thinking, and so the machine took the place of mans intelligence and was now substituted for mans problem solving.

For as much as the machine did solve many of man's problems effectively, the machines also randomly created other programs of intelligence, that man had now begun to adopt as his future vision in his pursuits towards building and creating his own reality, which would overtime prove to have negative results, and in being the causes of negative and erroneous effects on man's choice of direction toward reaching his ultimate goal.

λs it was during the innovative period, that it was man, who had invented the machines, and so it was that up until the point now and whilst during a new technological phase of progressions, whereupon the machines had now begun to make machines, as to whether this was to be seen as a logical, or illogical progression, except that what followed next during this period of innovation, is that the machines had now begun to make man, or rather modified man to the point that he would be assigned a programmable number, that would take the form of a digital component, that was assigned and injected into the body of man and wo-man.

As it was during this technological experiment, that man was no longer to be assigned a first name or a surname, but was instead assigned a number, and so it was this directive that caused a distinct rift between man, and other men and wo-men, and so began the fallout, between those who were in favor of this Digital Angel Chip Implant of DNA Biometrics, and of those who were decidedly against it, and staunchly remained in favor of man's natural abilities to sustain his and her own growth of development unaided by the intervention of the machines.

As it was also during this new age directive protocol, that the harvesting of organs from the deceased were also now being recycled for the purposes of implanting, and for the purpose of the cloning of a perfect species, which had brought into bearance the ethical question, of what it is, or what it is not, to be human, as man had by now reached a point of no return, as this fork in the road had prompted the grouping of individuals to be assigned and placed into their own respective classifications according to their place and the time of their birth.

Although at this stage, births were still being registered, and only first names and numbers were beings issued as a point of historical reference and identification, but consequently what was to follow, was the copying and then the cloning of every birth leading up to this new millennia, so that in any event, albeit, that if any humans were to succumb to death or even die unpredictably during this program, then the machine could quite easily harvest and replace by an exact and perfect copy of the deceased.

As man and wo-man was now becoming desensitized to themselves and their environment, as man and wo-man by now had become predisposed to the introduction of these measures, as their ideas had strayed far and wide from what the Beings of the Sky world had originally shared with them, and so the idea of being called man-one or woman-one, or man-two and woman-two, was an idea that quickly gathered pace and momentum, and yet those with adverse exceptions to such draconian measures being implemented, were made to be omitted from the program, and so went underground, or formed other allied groups so as to avoid this new and dark reality.

Even though ironically the idea that these machines were of an origin previously designed by man, many of whom, who were by now, either very old, or had been classified as dead, or deceased, and so by the time that this new age had taken root, so it was that no one could have known, or even have imagined, or predicted, that in their initial designs of reaching the Sky world, that this technology would now be used to redirect man and wo-man to an alternative reality and outcome concerning his own intended future.

As it was from that point onwards that the classifications and the groups of houses were formed, both nationally and internationally, for categorizing those at the time of their births to be assigned and allocated into their respective universal houses, as for those of whom were to challenge this directive, were by now being directed and referred to the 12 Houses, whereupon their elected delegate Obadiah, who also given the number 144, due to his knowledge and wisdom, and understanding of the Sky world Beings before the separation had lost its' unique connection.

As it was also he, that had also predicted some of the events of the coming age, and so instructed those of us who were motivated enough to plan and to prepare for a mass exodus of the Dome, and so to in paying heed to his warnings, along with the caution that we should remain vigilant in our preparedness for when the Sky Beings would one day return to be with us once again.

As it was under this guidance and this initiative, that we were advised to make provisions, and so began the construction of what would formerly be the first in a long line of successive word-ships, or w.o.r.ships, in recognition of our past relationship with the Sky Beings. As it was to be that these w.o.r.ships would transport those of us who were opposed to the directive of the machines, in that we should seek to serve out our existence and to ensure our future survival by taking our place amongst the planets and stars, and to even colonize the our nearest satellite, the Moon.

And so from now on, and from here on in, what indeed does a new day look like, as much we stand here beneath this new heaven and as much as we dwell upon this new earth, and yet what are we to do now that tomorrow has finally arrived, as much as this beacon of hope has lifted our spirits in becoming a fulfillment of a promise made, from the Beings of the Sky world now set before us upon this horizon, as we stand beneath and gaze up towards this new firmament above us, and yet so it would seem that this dream of the Angel Babies, has given birth to these fruits of creation, whilst sustaining the spirit, and the nature of this human soul.

EARTH DAY ONE: EXCELSIS DEO
λ.Ω ÉMANAŤΙΘNS OF BΛRBĒLŌ 1.É.D

Last night the stars were beaming, as I lay softly dreaming, a distant place inside of my soul, something so divine, Barbelo, the clouds above, kept on climbing, so much higher than the mountains, beneath the winds kept on blowing, as the eagle soared, forever sowing, Barbēlō.

Coming forth, giving life to each season, as they come and they go, for something that's breathing, inside of the Earth below, I thought I was dreaming, I thought I would never wake up, but something inside of me silently knows, Barbēlō, the rays of light, are surely blinding, inside of my mind, I'm surely finding, a river that's winding into the sea and beyond, as the shadows disappear, Barbēlō.

Isolated and lonely, from giving my testimony, and yet how did I get here, by transcending the stairway, as innocence tries to hide me, from the voices that guide me, its' the art of illusion, within a world of confusion, its' a tale and a fable, an Alien and an Angel, in and out of a black hole, through the portal of an ozone Barbēlō.

Somewhere in the universe, upon the edge of creation, where love holds the key unlocking the doors of inspiration, its' as if I've been waiting, within my own meditations, anticipating the Holy, A Spirit that knows me, Barbēlō.

λuthor
C.O.P.E – Citizen Of Planet Earth

OMEGA EARTH RECORDS: EXCELSIS DEO
λ.Ω CALENDAR YEAR 1.É.D

From out of the darkness comes the light, and yet for so long the darkness had prevailed over the human spirit, ever since the creation of the first world, as throughout the dawn of time, a lineage of distinctions were made to keep us at bay and separate from one another, and yet the human family, within its' own decline, had revealed itself to be one of partiality and at odds and ends with itself.

λs it is only through our indifference, or when we are challenged, do we truly see that our humanity is one of the same accord, in knowing full well, that as we rise above and move beyond the darkness of principalities, that this newly created world, that we have come to inherit, makes no distinctions between us, as it is the new Earth that has come to be redeemed for the benefit of the entire human family.

The beginning of a new cycle in life, with a divine purpose, a new life, of new cells forming, a healing presence of material sustenance, a ray of light for emanating with the representations of love and wisdom, a divine and golden light, symbolizing spiritual enlightenment, a majestic light, for the power, and the protection of faith, hope, strength and courage,

λ guiding light, as your soul is enlivened with the energies of peace, and calmness, and tranquility, that surpasses eternity, even after their passing away, as he that hath the power to create such a world, also hath the power to uncreate it, but not before he cleave it unto his own bosom, and yet he that hath no desire, except to lead the world unto its' own destruction neither has no claim, nor no possession over it.

As was time immemorial, that after the end of the apocalypse, when all at once had become scarce throughout the world, so the time had come to make such music, and to plant the corn, and to build a world worthy his own, even with ten fingers and with ten toes, who amongst us would plant the seed, and who amongst us would clothe the naked with such heavenly garments, and who take it upon him or herself to write these words, and who amongst us with sticks and stones, shall lay the foundations of thy cornerstone.

As for those of us, who have had a vision of the son, witnessed through the silvery eyes of such unfailing strength, in openly obeying the honest words that have fallen upon the ears of thy faithful emerald, issued forth from the will of thy mouth, entwining the decorations of the pearls mounted upon thy purple breastplate.

In praising the creator and the created, from such a hearty generator, that is besides the brownish fields of such enriched rubies, planted beneath the yellow rays of the sun, even when such hired hands are needed for reaping the gems of the peridote, by eliminating all the fears, and by abiding by the natural order, whilst fulfilling their stomachs, with the intuitions of such pink sapphires, whilst being granted in yielding such blessings of abundance.

As much as a defender, and a judge, along with the strength of his backbone, and the purity a blue opal of hope, fit for the girdle of thy pelvis, enriched with the power of thy red topaz, in bringing about such good fortunes of overstanding, if only to strengthen thy thigh, and to uncloud the grayness of thy turquoise mind, in order to straighten out, and to forwardly pursue, the wisdom of thy protections, to strengthen thy hip against a hindrance let loose, even as the one above is also the one below.

Whilst being decorated and adorned, with a green garnet, and such symbols of thy love, if only to wonder the inspirations of a creative spirit and imaginative mind, as such are the blessings, from perfection unto perfection, with a nose for the bright white beautiful fragrances, set against the calm winds of thine own amethyst, along with the lightheartedness, to skip, and to diligently jump and dance, the productivity of the black foot, besides the ever youthful intelligent waters, and the purity of thy aquamarine.

So Put away the former things, for the latter things have already taken place, and the bitter sting of death has also already lost its' bitter taste, and has no venom to speak of, and as of yet, the 11th hour has also proceeded to come and go, and so as of now, we have already excelled within our will at Godspeed, to go and to live and to dwell in and amongst the realm of the Holy Spirit.

UPON THE RESTORATION OF: CREATION
λ.Ω JUBĬLAŤΘN 1.É.Đ

For as much as a single day may consist of 24 equal hours, between sunrise and sunset, as much as it may be divided into 12 equal parts, then so shall it be, that the one thing that shall remain to abide with us, is that one day with the Lord, is likened unto a thousand years, and yet a thousand for years, to live upon this new Earth, is likened unto one day.

Even as we stand before the Sun has arisen, so soon shall it be, that all such things shall come to pass, inasmuch that we are permitted to live, and to inhabit and to dwell within this new world, then so shall it be, that upon its' renewal and restoration, whereby the delivery of our prayers and invocations are fulfilled and answered, upon this day of all days.

λnd so shall it be duly noted and observed, that upon this morning, and whatsoever shall come to follow by this afternoon, and lastly whatsoever shall come to follow upon this evening, and whatever is given cause to have happened, has already come to happen, and whatsoever shall come to pass, has already come to pass.

For as much as the voices within the wilderness are loud, still the voice within your heart, is much louder, and as much as they may whisper words into your ear, still the voice of clarity, makes all things much clearer, for as much as the voices, within the void, attempt to bring you down, still the voice of thee Almighty, speaks much bolder, whilst giving glory to his name, Sánctus, Hosánna, Glória in Excélsis Deo.

λuthor
L.O.V.E – Life's Omnipotent Virtuous Entity

MARANATHA: EXCELSIS DEO
λ.Ω ΛN ΛGÉ Λ TIMÉ ΘF ΛÉΘNS 1.É.Đ

The ending of the world is just beginning, and yet the beginning of the world has hardly begun, and yet even throughout the ages and within this aeon of time, even the Earth has stood still to witness the countless number of generations, passing through this myriad of historical and successive events, that have brought us thus far, and yet who would of thought, or even believed that such a dream was being dreamt, by none other than that of a baby, or indeed by the Angel Babies.

And yet even if you ask me about my thoughts, then I shall share my ideas with you, and if you ask me about my beliefs, then I shall share my faith with you, however I cannot tell you what to think about this world in which we all live, and I cannot tell you what to believe within this world that we all inhabit.

However, as much as we are all evolving, and adapting, and changing and transitioning, if not from one day, then from one moment to the next, and yet as precious and as fragile as life may be, still it seems that we are only here for a short and brief, and yet infinite amount of time, if only to experience and to share the simplest of things, if not our love, within this world.

And yet as of when the first fruits come forth, so too is it also, that what may be the cause of the cries of the first newly born, is either because, it is their first innocent gaze upon the rays of sunlight, or simply perhaps, like old souls, they have been here before, and so therefore they are reminded, as they recollect in knowing all of the events that are bound to come and to follow.

WHY THE DEATH OF DEATH: IS NOT DEATH
λ.Ω ŤHÉ SPIRIT ŤHÉ SOUL ŤHÉ BODY 1.É.Đ

Because of the Spirit, the Soul is animated

Because of the Spirit, the Soul bears consciousness

Because of the Spirit, the Soul is emotional

Because of the Spirit, the Soul yields breath

Because of the Soul, the Spirit is ignited

Because of the Soul, the Spirit has cognition

Because of the Soul, the Spirit is empowered

Because of the Soul, the Body has Life

Because of the Body, the Soul engages the Heart

Because of the Body, the Spirit engages the Mind

λuthor
O.A.O – Over And Out

REFERÉNCE

Edward Tyler (1832 - 1917)
A Soul - **Anima**
R. R. Marett (1866 - 1943)
A Soul – **Animism / Animatism**
Algonquian Indians (A Soul - Otahchuk)
Tetra Valley - (Fictional Four Sided Valley)
Samsara (A Former life influences the present one)
Jiva (Hindu term for the Personal Soul or Being)
Cavea - (Cage Of The Soul In The Sea)
Kali Ma - (Hindu Supreme Goddess or Black Earth Mother)
Mercidiah (Earth Mother)
Josephine (Younger Fictional Earth Mother)
Papiosa - (Depicting Good and Evil)
Men Shen - (Taoist Interpretation/Guardians of the Door)
Hark the Herald - (The listening Angel)
Angel Simeon - (The Protecting Angel)
Pablo the Immortal - (The Eternal Angel)
Angel Ophlyn - (The Fallen Angel)
Angel Ruen - (The Avenging Angel)
Angel Stefan - (The Angel Of Love)
Angel Leoine - (Bastion & Sentient)
Angel of Justice - (Figuratively)
Angel of Mercy - (Figuratively)
Nejeru - (New Jerusalem)
Golden Dawn - (The Future Arising Sun)
Proarkhe the Arkhe - (Presence Of The Almighty)
Angel Haven (Successor To Hark The Herald Angel)
Anahita - (Earth Mother of Selah/Daughter Of Papiosa & Leoine)
Angel Nephi (Son Of Ophlyn & Kali Ma/Father Of Selah)
Angel E' Nocturnālis - (Depicting Darkness)
Angel E'diurnālis - (Depicting Light)
Manoo - (Son Of Angel Ruen & Earth Mother Uama)
Angel An'jela - (A Muse & Sentinel)
Obadiah 144 - (Prophet And Visionary)
Empyrean – (Sky world/Heaven)
Ophanim (Throne Of God/Emerald Green)

PURPORTED

(Λngel-Trans-Lation)

So It Is
Uck-Han-Dudullud
I Declare It Is So
Dudullud-Uck-Han.♡

Angelus Domini

INSPIRIT*ASPIRE*ESPRIT*INSPIRE

A **Tao.House** Product

Ťhə ʌNĠƏL ʙʌʙĬƏS XVI

Unorthodox Excelsis Deo

Valentine Fountain of Love Ministry

Info contact: ***tao.house@live.co.uk***

Copyright: Clive Alando Taylor 2022

Printed in the United States
by Baker & Taylor Publisher Services